Adult Coloring Stress Relief

with Calming Card Games

Diamonds

Copyright © Leaves of Gold Press 2015

All rights reserved. No part of this book may be reproduced or transmitted by any person or entity (including Google, Amazon or similar organisations) in any form or by any means, electronic or mechanical, including photocopying, recording or by any information storage and retrieval system, without prior permission in writing from the publisher.

Creator: Leaves of Gold Press - author.

Title: Adult coloring stress relief with calming card games: diamonds /
Leaves of Gold Press ;
Elizabeth Alger, illustrator.
Series: Adult coloring stress relief ; 4
ISBN: 9781925110883 (paperback)
Target Audience: Adult.

Image on reverse of cards: 'Pimpernel' by William Morris

BISAC categories:
Self-Help / Self-Management / Stress Management
Self-Help : Creativity
Body, Mind & Spirit / Mindfulness & Meditation

Scan the QR code to visit Leaves of Gold Press

ABN 67 099 575 078
PO Box 9113, Brighton, 3186, Victoria, Australia
www.leavesofgoldpress.com

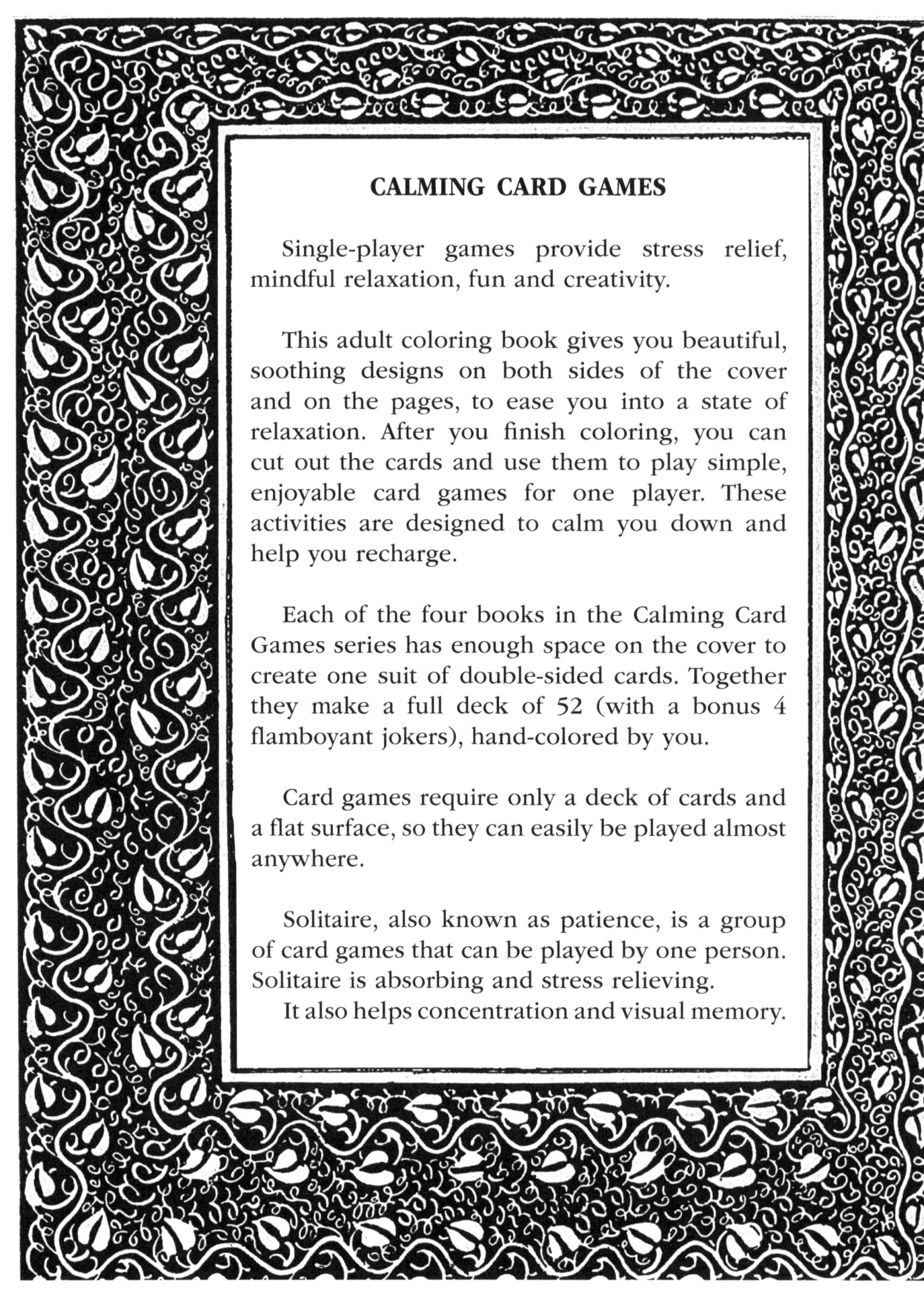

CALMING CARD GAMES

Single-player games provide stress relief, mindful relaxation, fun and creativity.

This adult coloring book gives you beautiful, soothing designs on both sides of the cover and on the pages, to ease you into a state of relaxation. After you finish coloring, you can cut out the cards and use them to play simple, enjoyable card games for one player. These activities are designed to calm you down and help you recharge.

Each of the four books in the Calming Card Games series has enough space on the cover to create one suit of double-sided cards. Together they make a full deck of 52 (with a bonus 4 flamboyant jokers), hand-colored by you.

Card games require only a deck of cards and a flat surface, so they can easily be played almost anywhere.

Solitaire, also known as patience, is a group of card games that can be played by one person. Solitaire is absorbing and stress relieving.
It also helps concentration and visual memory.

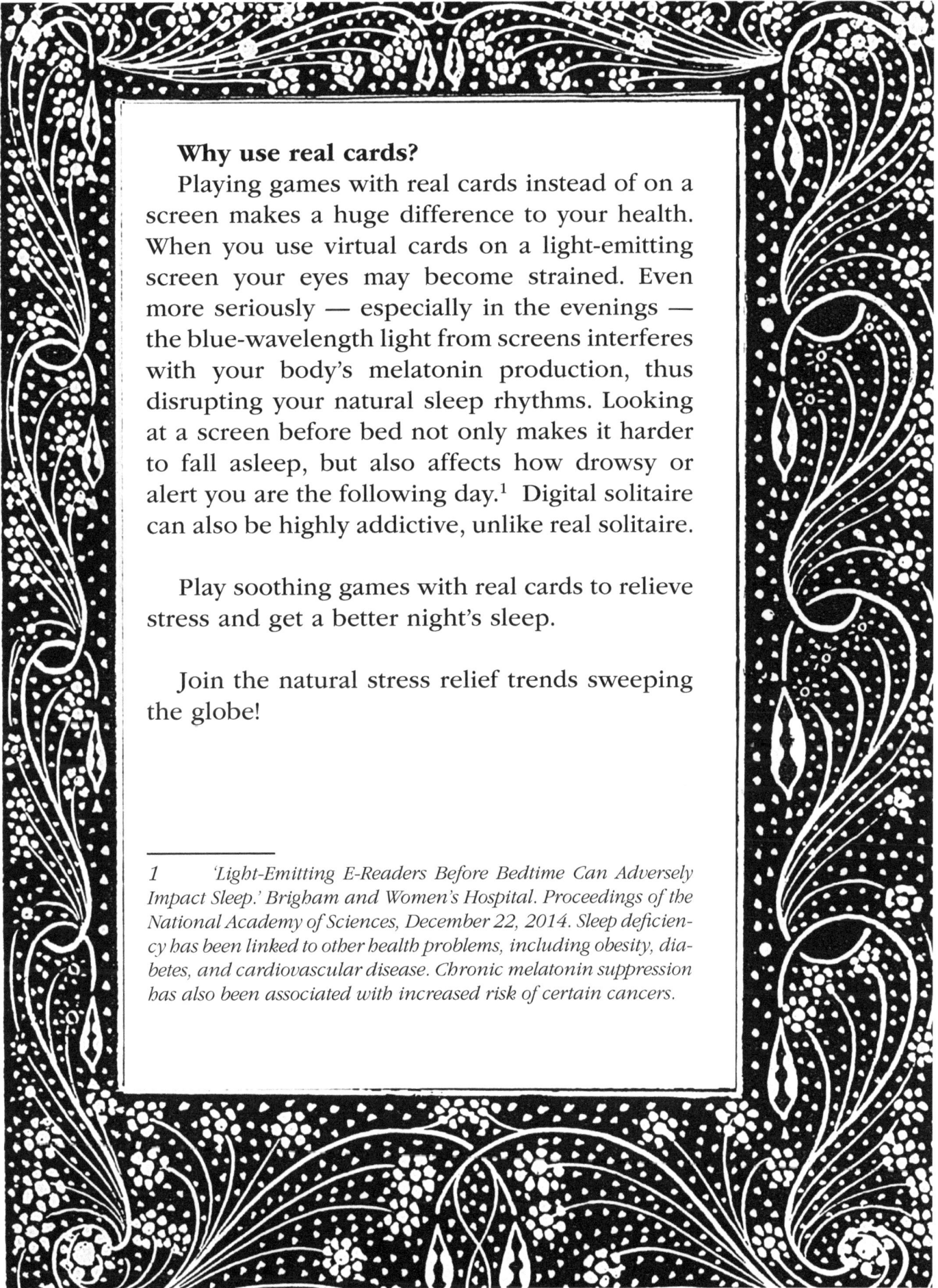

Why use real cards?

Playing games with real cards instead of on a screen makes a huge difference to your health. When you use virtual cards on a light-emitting screen your eyes may become strained. Even more seriously — especially in the evenings — the blue-wavelength light from screens interferes with your body's melatonin production, thus disrupting your natural sleep rhythms. Looking at a screen before bed not only makes it harder to fall asleep, but also affects how drowsy or alert you are the following day.[1] Digital solitaire can also be highly addictive, unlike real solitaire.

Play soothing games with real cards to relieve stress and get a better night's sleep.

Join the natural stress relief trends sweeping the globe!

---

1   'Light-Emitting E-Readers Before Bedtime Can Adversely Impact Sleep.' Brigham and Women's Hospital. *Proceedings of the National Academy of Sciences, December 22, 2014. Sleep deficiency has been linked to other health problems, including obesity, diabetes, and cardiovascular disease. Chronic melatonin suppression has also been associated with increased risk of certain cancers.*

♦ THE SUIT OF DIAMONDS ♦

The set of 52 French playing cards is the most popular European deck. This comprises thirteen numerals of each of the four French suits; clubs, diamonds, hearts and spades. Each suit includes three 'court' or 'face' cards; king, queen and jack.

The Suit of Diamonds is derived from the Suit of Coins. The French converted them to tiles, or diamonds (*carreaux*).

In tarot, diamonds corresponds to pentacles, coins, rings or discs. The element of diamonds is earth, and the Suit of Pentacles is associated with money, risk and excitement.

The Suit of Diamonds may represent the feudal class of burghers (middle-class citizens).

It also corresponds to the Swiss-German Suit of Bells (*Schellen*).

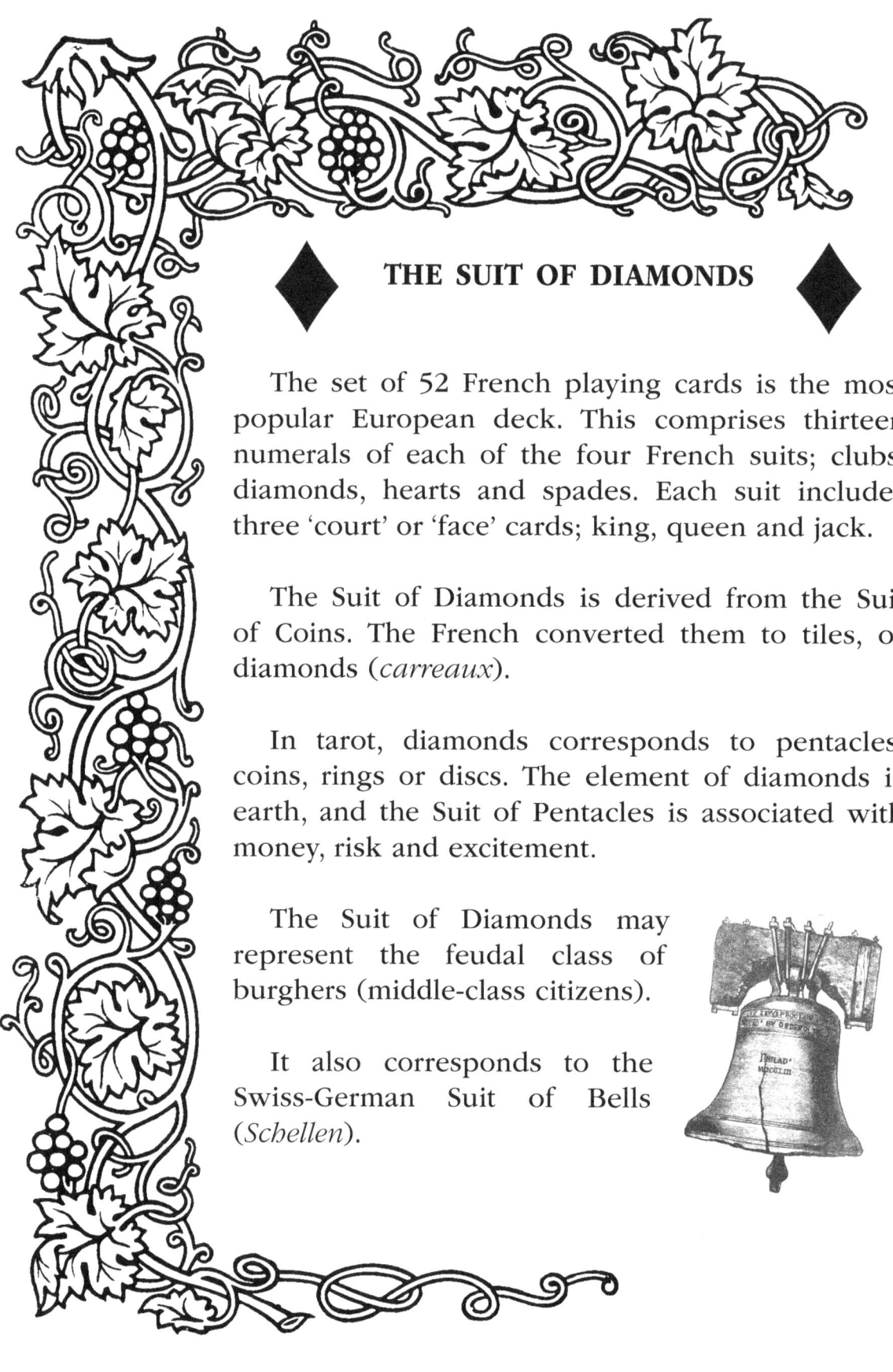

SOLITAIRE OR PATIENCE

Games of solitaire/patience generally involve re-arranging a layout of cards (called a 'tableau') with the aim of sorting them in some way.

There is a vast array of variations in one-player card games. The rules vary from simple to quite complex. Some use more than one deck of cards. This series of books, 'Adult Coloring Stress Relief with Calming Card Games' contains instructions for several of the most popular and relaxing games of solitaire, including:

- Klondike
- Accordion
- Flower Garden
- Spiderette
- Pyramid

Pyramid Solitaire

With Pyramid you match cards that add up to 13 and work your way to the top of the playing-card pyramid. This game is sometimes known as Solitaire 13.

Instructions follow.

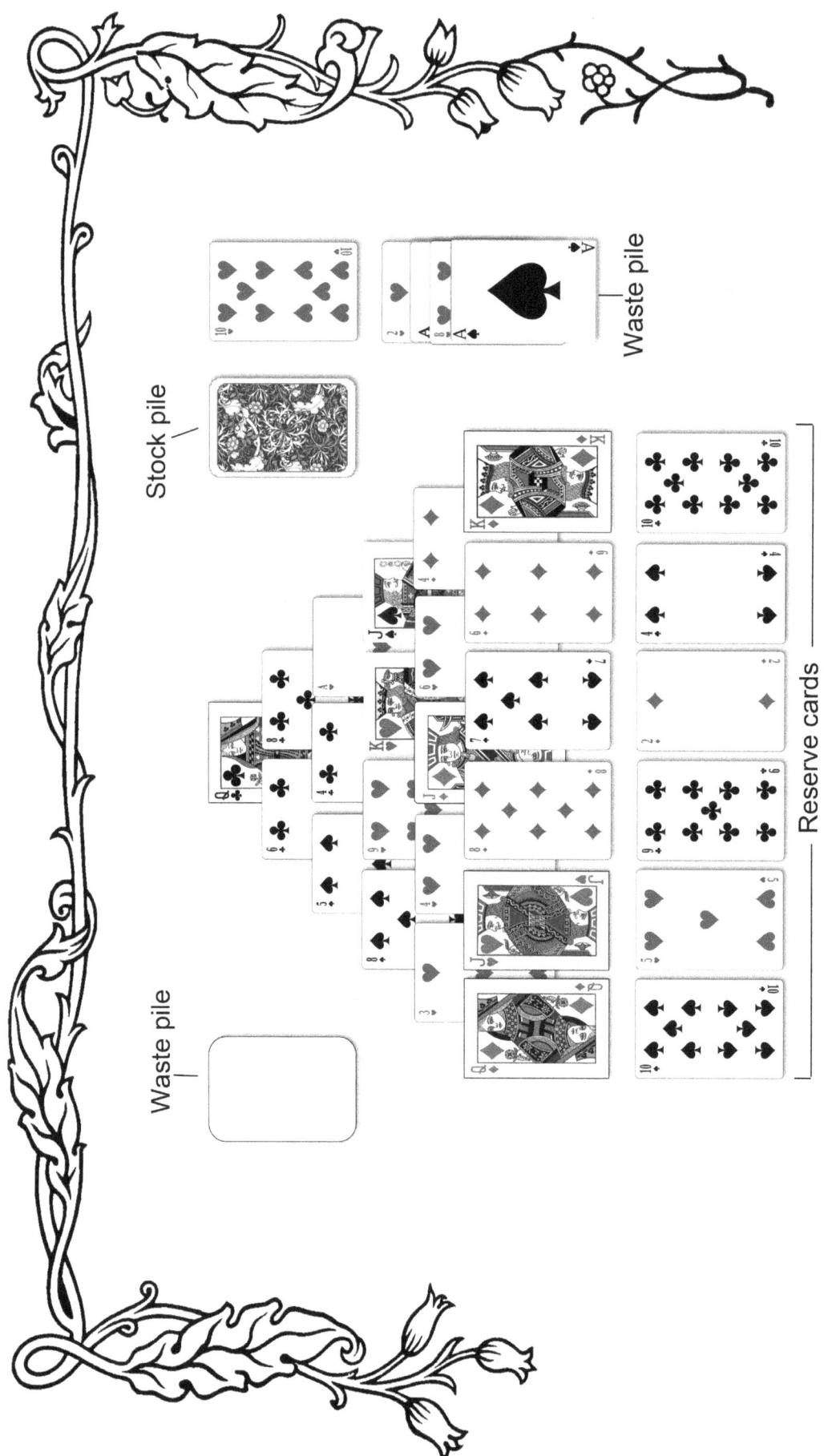

Layout for Pyramid Solitaire

PYRAMID SOLITAIRE

Pyramid is a one-player game with simple rules. A standard deck of 52 cards is used, and you can play a hand in only a few minutes.

The aim of the game is to remove all of the cards from the pyramid.

Setup

Shuffle the deck. Deal out the cards to form a pyramid, beginning with one card in the top row, then just below it a row of two cards, then a row of three and so on, down to the final row of seven cards. Each row should overlap the preceding row.

When you've finished laying out the pyramid it will contain a total of 28 cards.

Place the remaining cards in a single stack face-down on the table. This pile becomes the 'stock' or 'draw' pile.

Gameplay

Turn over cards from the stock pile, one by one. If a card from the stock pile is not able to be used, place it face-up next to the stock pile. Each unusable card should cover up the previous unusable face-up card from the stock pile. You can use these cards later in the game, but only if they are the top, uncovered card.

When the numbers on two of your revealed cards total 13, you can move them to the 'waste' pile.

It is optional whether you discard a card to the waste pile or not. Sometimes it will be more strategically advantageous to keep the card.

Cards in the pyramid are considered to be 'revealed' if no other cards are overlapping them. Only one card from the draw pile is 'revealed' at any point in the game. For example the most recent stock pile card you have flipped over is the only card from the stock pile that is 'revealed'.

Some examples of play:

If a 9 and a 4 are both revealed in the pyramid, they can be discarded to the waste pile. If a 5 is revealed in the pyramid and an 8 is revealed after being turned face-up from the stock pile, you can discard them, too.

Card values
- Aces are worth 1
- Jacks are worth 11
- Queens are worth 12
- Kings are worth 13 and can be discarded by themselves.

This means that the card-pairings you can discard are:

King – by itself
Queen + ace
Jack + 2
10 + 3
9 + 4
8 + 5
7 + 6

Winning

The game finished when you have removed every card from the pyramid or when you have used up all the cards in the stock pile — whichever happens first.

If you can manage to remove all of the cards from the pyramid, you win.

Variation

Instead of flipping over cards from the stock pile one at a time, turn them over in sets of three.

Lay the first set of three on the table to begin three separate piles. After that, when you draw more cards you should spread the three new cards over these three piles. The order in which you place cards on the piles should stay the same throughout the game.

ADULT COLORING STRESS RELIEF: THE SERIES

Book 1: Adult Coloring Stress Relief with Calming Paper Crafts

Book 2: Adult Coloring Stress Relief with Calming Card Games: Spades

Book 3: Adult Coloring Stress Relief with Calming Card Games: Hearts

Book 4: Adult Coloring Stress Relief with Calming Card Games: Diamonds

Book 5: Adult Coloring Stress Relief with Calming Card Games: Clubs

IS FOOD MAKING YOU SICK?

People all over the world suffer from histamine intolerance without being aware of it.

We itch, sneeze, suffer from joint pain, inflammation, sleep disorders, irritability, anxiety, bowel disease, diarrhea, flatulence, stomach pain, heartburn and acid reflux, nausea, bloating and other digestive problems, eczema, psoriasis, tissue swelling, urticaria (hives), itching skin, itching scalp, sinusitis, runny nose, puffy eyes, hay fever, asthma, and breathing difficulties, or endure tension headaches, migraines, fuzzy thinking, dizziness, irregular heartbeat, painful periods (women), sudden drops in blood pressure, faintness or flushing.

Symptoms may endure throughout our entire lives if we continue to consume large amounts of histamine without knowing it. Histamine is colorless, odorless and tasteless — undetectable except by scientific analysis, and yet crucial to our well-being. Individual histamine tolerance thresholds vary greatly.

The good news is, if we can understand what is happening and why, we can treat or prevent this widely unrecognized condition. By far the best way to treat histamine intolerance (HIT) is with diet. All foods with the potential to raise histamine levels should be avoided until your health improves significantly.

This book discusses HIT in depth, including causes, symptoms and therapies, backed by scientific research. Along with a list of foods to help HIT sufferers, it includes a wide range of recipes for everything from entrées to desserts.

Find out more at www.low-histamine.com

THE SLEEP-INDUCING BEDTIME STORY

Children sometimes find it hard to get to sleep.

What if you could read them a bedtime story incorporating powerful psychological methods to help them fall asleep quickly, easily and without drugs?

Psychological sleep induction techniques include:
- putting aside your thoughts until the following day
- breathing deeply
- slowing down
- imagining a descent with the sensation of sinking
- progressive muscle relaxation
- using sleep-triggering words
- visualizing a safe and peaceful place
- employing the 'infectiousness' of yawning.

Such methods are well-known and can be found in libraries or by searching for 'psychological sleep techniques' on the Internet.

This book also uses the hypnotic power of rhyme and rhythm. Songs and lullabies have traditionally been used to lull children to sleep. 'Hypnotic' poetry works in much the same way.

The poems in this book are in the relaxing, calming rhythm called 3/4 time, better known as 'waltz time'. All parents know that gentle, rocking rhythms can soothe a child.

The rhyming is as important as the rhythm.

Children love poems that rhyme. For them, rhyming words make poetry fun and memorable. Just as children respond to Forssen Ehrlin's sleep-inducing story of Roger the Rabbit (the inspiration for this book), so they can fall asleep while listening to the tale of Misti the Kitty.

 # 1 New Release on Amazon in 'Sleep Disorders'.

www.ingramcontent.com/pod-product-compliance
Lightning Source LLC
LaVergne TN
LVHW070951070426
835507LV00030B/3491